Reading Ideas Ready to Use!
for K-6 Educators

(includes reproducible pages)

by

Barbara Jean Gruber

illustrator Lynn Conklin Power

Copyright© 1983 Frank Schaffer Publications, Inc.
All rights reserved - Printed in the U.S.A.
Published by **Frank Schaffer Publications, Inc.**
1028 Via Mirabel, Palos Verdes Estates, California 90274

ISBN #0-86734-049-5

Table of Contents

Getting Ready to Read

Make sure your students have a positive attitude about reading right from the start! On the following pages, you'll find ideas for creating a classroom environment that conveys the message: "Reading Is Fun!" Try some of the suggested readiness activities too. Students will enjoy learning as they develop fundamental reading skills.

Creating the right atmosphere

Message Strips

For primary classrooms:

Label a variety of classroom objects. Cut strips of construction paper or use sentence strips to post messages around the room. Start with a few strips. Read them to the class. Add more strips on a regular basis. Children will notice the new messages and will want to know what they say. After you read the message strips to your class, have students read them to each other.

Announcements

For grades 2-6:

Pick a spot on the chalkboard where you will write important daily announcements. Or, post messages on the bulletin board for students to read.

Creating the right atmosphere

Read & Share

Divide a bulletin board so you have enough sections for each child in your class. .
(Leave an extra space for yourself too!) Write each student's name in a section on the bulletin board. Students may post interesting items that they have read and would like the rest of the class to read. You will amass a wonderful collection of notes, letters, cartoons, greeting cards, clippings from magazines and newspapers, as well as samples of children's writing. Encourage students to change their bulletin board items frequently.

Leave extra spaces for new students who are bound to join your class!

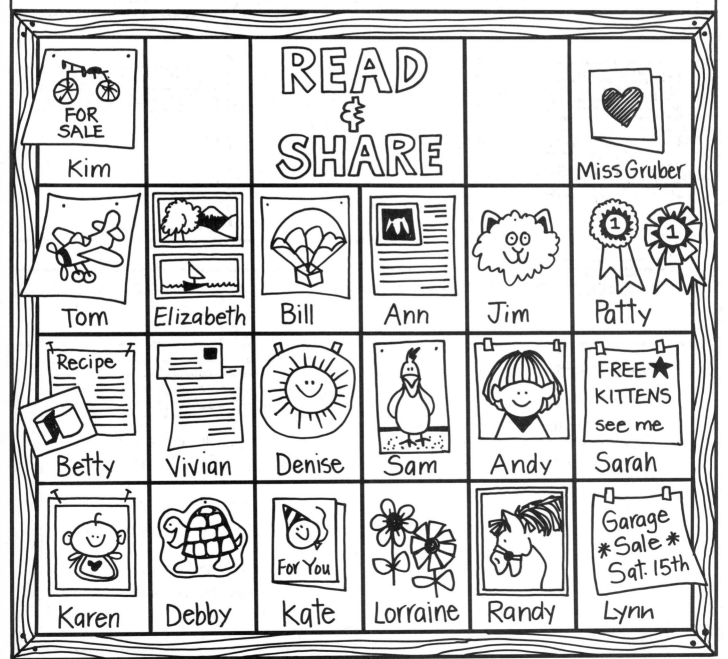

Creating the right atmosphere

Create a "Reading Is Fun" atmosphere in your classroom . . .

The Book Box

Place several paperback books that students like to read in the Book Box. Tell students they may each borrow a book from the box if they put in one of their own paperback books. Students can use books from the Book Box for:

- silent reading period
- book reports
- reading for enjoyment

Share books from the Book Box with students from other classrooms.

Start a paperback and magazine exchange in the teachers' lounge too!

Instant Storybooks

Accumulate copies of basal readers that are no longer used in your school's reading program. If possible, collect old basals from both the grade level below and above your grade.

Tear the books apart, story by story. Use tagboard to make front and back covers. Staple together to make individual storybooks. Give each student a story to read. Have students decorate the book covers to illustrate the stories.

This is a terrific way to gather lots of books with controlled vocabulary levels for your classroom library.

Creating the right atmosphere

Silent Reading

Silent reading time is a special time for your students to relax and enjoy books. Kindergarten students like picture books while older students may prefer reading books that take several weeks to finish. Hang a "Do Not Disturb" sign on the outside of your classroom door and enjoy silent reading for a few minutes every day. Be sure **you** read a book too!

Some suggestions for a successful silent reading program:

- Make sure you have a variety of books available in your classroom library.

- Establish a specific amount of time for each silent reading period. Start with a short time period and gradually lengthen it. Four minutes for primary students and 10 minutes for intermediate students may be an appropriate starting point.

- Set a few rules to ensure that the time is spent reading. For instance, students should select their silent reading materials beforehand. They simply take the books out of their desks and start reading when it's time for silent reading. You may want to insist that everyone stays in their seats during the silent reading time.

- Set aside time after the silent reading period for students to share information about the books they are reading with the class.

Suggest to parents that the family establish a silent reading time at home!

Some students enjoy keeping track of their reading progress. Use the reproducible reading log on page 47.

Organize Your Classroom Library

Sort out your paperback books and store them in shoe boxes. Write a category label on each shoe box. Students can quickly locate the book they want to read.

Ask students to organize the classroom library for you during a rainy-day indoor recess.

Prolong the life of your paperbacks. Cover them with clear plastic (i.e., Contac®) adhesive.

Promote the joy of reading

It Pays to Advertise

Borrow 10 books from the school library. Select an assortment of books such as a travel book, an adventure story, a poetry book, a story about a famous person, etc. Display the books on a special table in your classroom and tell students not to touch them. Inform students that all the books are from the school library and you will return them at the end of the week. Whenever you have a minute or two before the bell rings, pick up one of the books and read a short segment or show a picture from it. You are, in effect, doing a commercial for the book. Try to "advertise" all 10 books by the end of the week. Return them to the school library and choose 10 books for the next week. You will be amazed when you see your students dashing to the library to check out the books you have advertised!

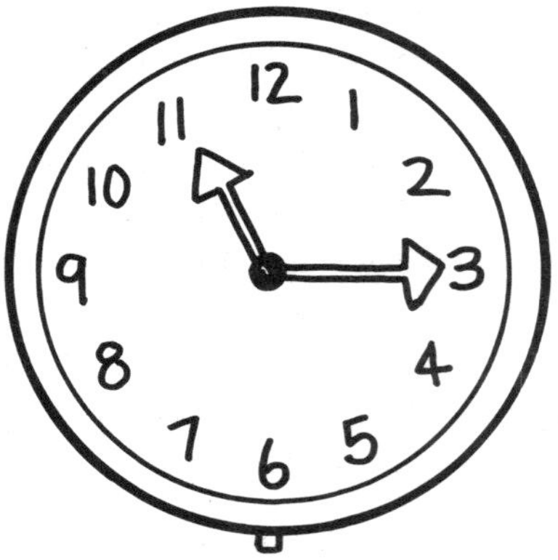

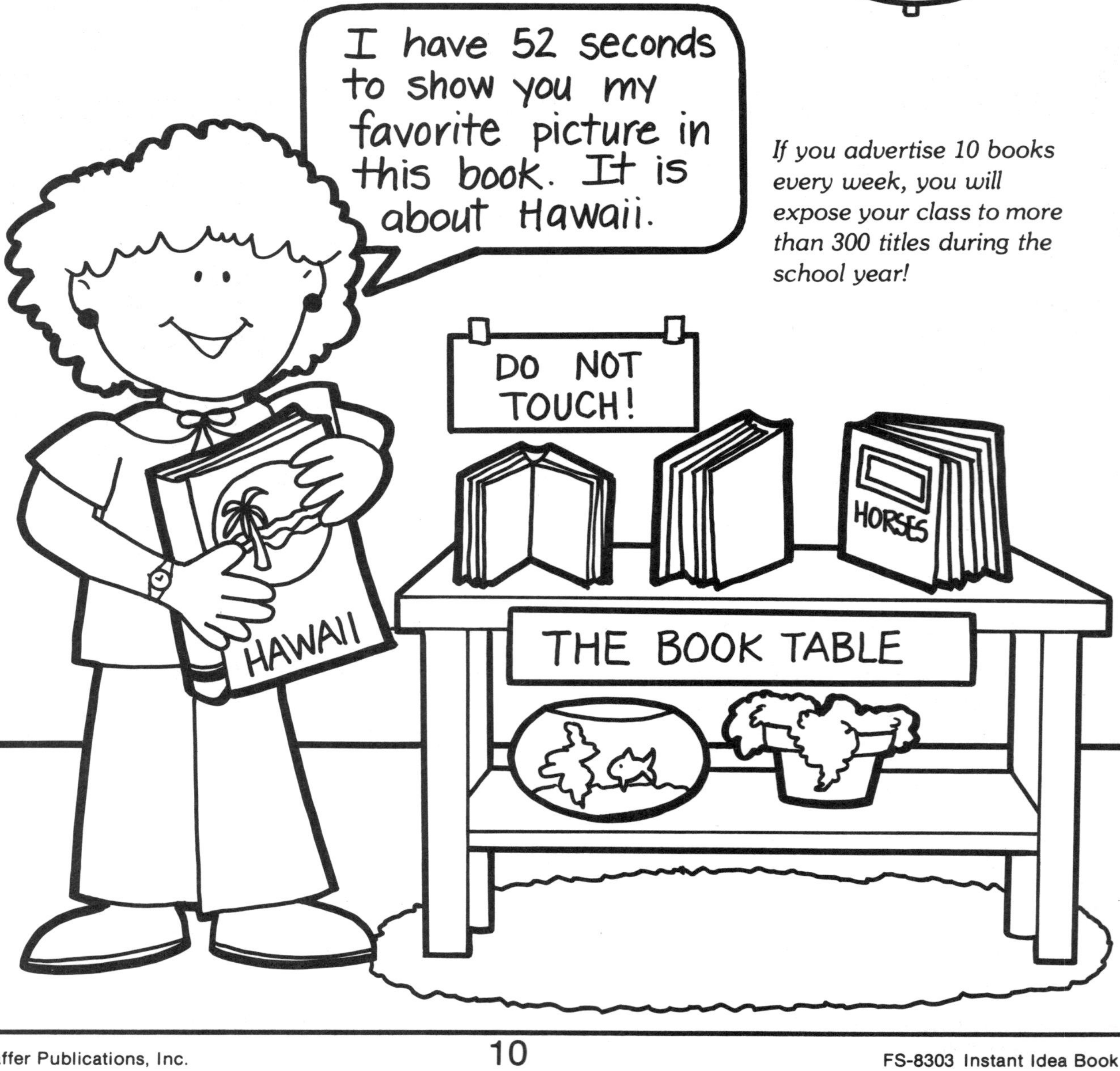
I have 52 seconds to show you my favorite picture in this book. It is about Hawaii.
DO NOT TOUCH!
HAWAII
HORSES
THE BOOK TABLE

If you advertise 10 books every week, you will expose your class to more than 300 titles during the school year!

Reading aloud ✓

Read to your class . . . for the fun of it!

Poetry

Read selected poems to your class each week. Encourage students to bring poetry books to share with the class. If your students especially enjoy a particular poem, write the poem on a large piece of butcher paper. Appoint a student to illustrate the poem or add a colorful border. Then post the poem in the classroom. A good place for your "poetry wall" is under the chalk ledge. Students will enjoy reading the poems themselves.

Post poems written by your students too!

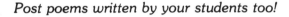

Books

Read a chapter a day to your students from a popular book. Ask other teachers or the school librarian for suggestions. Reading to your class is a pleasant experience for both you and your students. It expands listening vocabulary and increases student interest in reading.

Reading suggestions to share with parents:

- Read to your children every day.

- Give children a special place to keep their books.

- Help children obtain a public library card. Find out about special programs the public library sponsors for school-age children. Encourage children to visit the library often. Help them select interesting books to read.

- Give books to children as gifts. Ask your school librarian to compile a list of appropriate titles that you can send home for parents.

- Encourage children to give books as gifts to other children.

- Teach children to respect books and treat them with care.

Student-made books

✓ Student-Created Books

Books created by your reading readiness students . . .

Student-made books add fun and excitement to your reading program. Student-created books can be:

- placed in your classroom library

- shared with other classrooms

- taken home and shared with the student's family.

Use three pieces of 12″ x 18″ construction paper to make a booklet for each student. Use one color for the cover sheet and a different (light) color for the booklet pages. Fold and staple the paper as shown.

12″ x 18″ construction paper

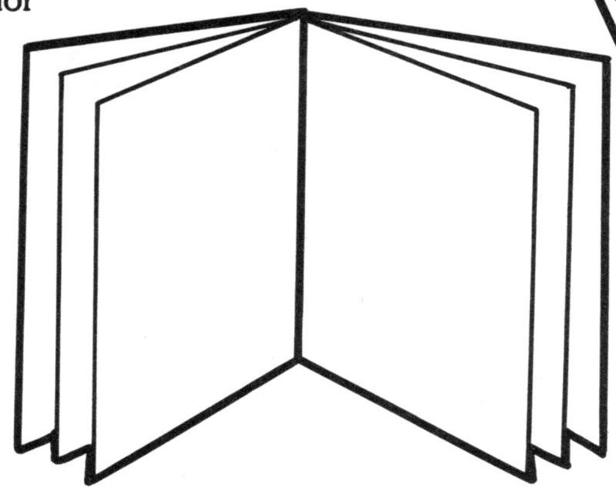

Fold and staple. Make two covers and eight pages.

Each student selects a subject for the book: animals, food, favorite things, etc. If the book is about animals, for example, the student will need to cut out eight animal pictures from old magazines. Pictures are pasted in the book, one picture per page. While students are working on their books, the teacher circulates and writes a sentence on each page. The sentence should be repetitive except for one or two words so students can "read" their books. Help children create titles for their books. Write the title and the student's name on the front cover of each book. The front and back covers can be decorated by the author.

Ideas for books:
- animals
- people
- places
- favorite things

Suggestions for text:
- Look at the . . .
- I like the . . .
- See the . . .

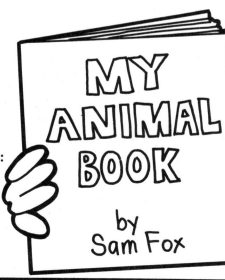

See the dog. See the pig.

inside

Reading activities for beginners

Words to Learn

Challenging activities to give your beginning readers a great start!

- Make a color word dictionary and a number word dictionary for each student. They can use these dictionaries to follow directions that require reading color and number words.

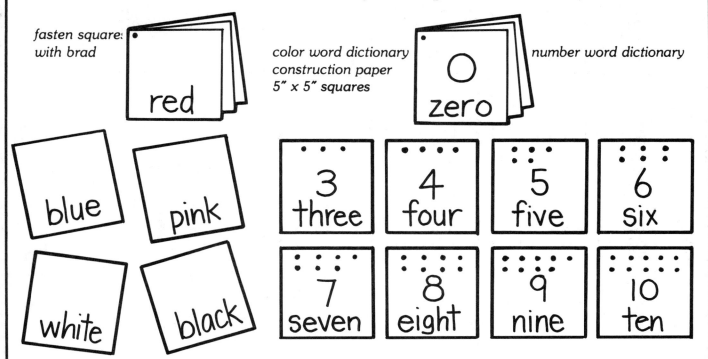

fasten squares with brad

color word dictionary construction paper 5" x 5" squares

number word dictionary

red, blue, pink, white, black

0 zero, 3 three, 4 four, 5 five, 6 six, 7 seven, 8 eight, 9 nine, 10 ten

- Duplicate the "Words to Learn" worksheet on page 14. Encourage students to take it home for practice and review. Or, you can staple or paste the completed worksheet in each child's folder or reading workbook. Students can refer to it when they need help.

That's 8, e-i-g-h-t.

Thanks!

Words to Learn

Words to Learn

Color Words — Color the ▢

red	blue	yellow	white	black	orange	purple	green	brown

Number Words — Trace the number.

0　1　2　3　4　5　6　7　8　9　10

zero　one　two　three　four　five　six　seven　eight　nine　ten

Words that tell me what to do — Trace the word.

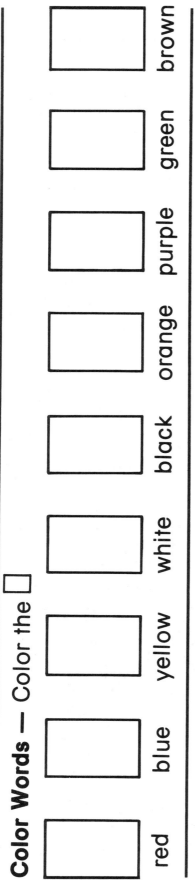

color

cut

paste

FS-8303 Instant Idea Book

Reading activities for beginners

Class Books

• Make a class book. Show a film, read a story or take a walk around the school to develop a theme for the class book. If your class reads a book about dinosaurs, for example, have each child draw a picture to illustrate the book. As students are working on their pictures, circulate around the room and ask each student what his or her picture is about. Write a sentence dictated by the child below the picture. Collect all the pictures and staple them together to make your class book. Select one student to decorate the cover of the book and place it in the class library.

12" x 18" art paper

Dinosaurs hatched from eggs. Don G.

Our Dinosaur Book
First Grade   Room 6

A little trick: Fold the bottom edge of student's papers. Unfold when you are ready to print the sentence. This prevents students from drawing in the sentence area.

Dinosaurs are now extinct.

FS-8303 Instant Idea Book

 **My ideas for reading readiness . . .**

FS-8303 Instant Idea Book

Vocabulary Development

Challenging activities that give you and your students relief from those dull vocabulary drills. Word games and visual aids are simple to make and provide valuable skill practice for students. All of the ideas are versatile in application and can be adapted to any classroom situation.

Word games that build vocabulary

Scrambled Words

A student-created activity that provides valuable reading and spelling practice!

How to make:

Assign a vocabulary word to each student.
(Or, use words from the list on page 19.)
Give everyone in your class an envelope and a
card or piece of heavy paper.

First, students write their words on the cards and
on the front of the envelopes. Then they cut apart
their words, letter by letter.

How to use:

Empty the scrambled letters from the envelope
onto the desk. Look at the word on the envelope
and then turn the envelope over so the word
cannot be seen.

Arrange the letters on the desk to spell the word.
Look at the word on the envelope and check
the spelling against the letters on the desk.

Put the letters back in the envelope and exchange
envelopes with another student.

Where to get free envelopes:

• Recycle used envelopes from your mail.

• Save return envelopes that come with "junk" mail.

• Ask parents and friends to save envelopes for you.

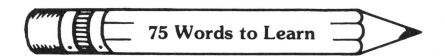

75 Words to Learn

Duplicate the list of high-frequency words on page 19. Give the list to students for practice
at home.

Use these words to make a set of flashcards for partner drill activites.
(Use the mini-flashcard format on page 27.)

75 WORDS TO LEARN

Students should learn to read and spell every word on this list. All of these words appear frequently in children's writing and reading materials.

1. I	21. in	41. one	61. than
2. a	22. into	42. my	62. that
3. an	23. or	43. are	63. this
4. and	24. for	44. must	64. our
5. any	25. on	45. may	65. will
6. at	26. up	46. by	66. with
7. as	27. of	47. other	67. was
8. he	28. have	48. would	68. were
9. we	29. so	49. people	69. what
10. be	30. to	50. men	70. when
11. she	31. can	51. said	71. who
12. had	32. do	52. only	72. which
13. has	33. made	53. time	73. us
14. his	34. you	54. now	74. but
15. him	35. your	55. more	75. told
16. her	36. all	56. the	
17. no	37. out	57. then	
18. is	38. not	58. they	
19. it	39. from	59. their	
20. its	40. been	60. there	

Categorizing to improve memory

Word Sorting

Categorizing words aids recall.

Students cut out small pictures from old workbooks and paste them on blank index cards. Label bags or boxes with category names. (See suggestions below.) Students categorize cards correctly.

Ideas:

- people, places, things
- plants, animals, people
- alive, not alive
- meat, fruit, vegetable
- colors, number words, sizes
- weather words, vehicles, places
- clothing, toys, furniture
- round, square, rectangular

Categorizing to improve memory

Categorize and illustrate

Make a list of words that can be sorted into three or four categories. The list of reading vocabulary words in the back of your teacher's manual is an excellent source. You can also use words from social studies and science units. Write each word on a blank index card and give one card to each student. Students must draw pictures to illustrate the word on their card. Write the category names on a large piece of butcher paper. Students paste their illustrated word cards under the proper category label.

Older students can do this activity in small groups. This is an excellent project for learning vocabulary words that relate to science or social studies units:

- meat, bread/cereal, vegetable/fruit, dairy
- mammal, fish, bird, reptile, amphibian
- food, clothing, shelter
- animals of forest, jungle, desert, farm

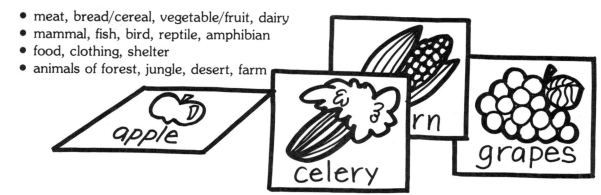

Vocabulary development can be fun

Vocabulary Bingo

A fun, once-a-week activity you can use all year long.

Write 36 words on the chalkboard every Monday morning. Use an assortment of words from your reading, spelling, science and social studies units.

Give each student a bingo worksheet. (Reproducible format is on page 23.) To save paper, make the worksheet reusable. Laminate it on a piece of tagboard and tell students to use wipe-off crayons.

Students select any combination of 24 words from the list on the board and write one word per square on the bingo grid.

When you are ready to play the bingo game, read a definition for one of the 36 words to the class. Any student who has that word on the grid crosses it out. The first student to cross out five words in a row (horizontally, vertically or diagonally) wins. Instead of using definitions for the words on the board, you can play synonym or antonym bingo.

Ideas:

- Play vocabulary bingo on a certain day each week. Tell students they must have their bingo grids ready-to-go (i.e., squares filled in with words from the board) by that day!

- If you write definitions on cards, you can let a student act as the "caller." Save sets of cards for reuse next year!

Vocabulary Bingo

FS-8303 Instant Idea Book

Visual aids to help boost vocabulary

Flip Books

Vocabulary words are taught most effectively when used in context. Students have a better understanding and recall when words are presented in sentences. After introducing words in context, you may want to have students make flip books to take home for practice.

For example, when teaching initial consonant substitution, write the word "cat" on the chalkboard and have each student copy it on a card or piece of construction paper. Then the student writes other initial consonants on half-sized cards and staples all the cards into a flip book.

Use for:

- root words
- plurals
- suffixes
- prefixes
- beginning blends

Have students read flip books to a partner.

Visual aids to help boost vocabulary

Mini-Flashcards

Mini-flashcards are perfect for vocabulary practice and review both at school and at home. Use the reproducible format on page 27. Duplicate plenty of copies so they will be ready to use!

How to use mini-flashcards with your students:

- Duplicate, then cut mini-flashcard into three vertical strips. Give each student a strip or nine blank mini-flashcards. Students write a reading vocabulary word on each card during the reading lesson. Then the strip can be cut apart, word by word, arranged in abc order and stapled into a pocket study book.

- Write words on the mini-flashcards that can be sorted into three categories such as:
  - people, places, things
  - nouns, verbs, adjectives

  Have students cut apart the word cards and paste them on 12″ x 18″ paper under the proper category headings. Or, if time is too short for a cut-and-paste activity, have students circle the "people" words with a red crayon, "places" words with yellow and "things" words with green.

More ideas on next page. →

©Frank Schaffer Publications, Inc.

FS-8303 Instant Idea Book

Visual aids to help boost vocabulary

- For beginning readers: Duplicate enough copies of the mini-flashcard worksheet for each student. When a student learns a new word, print it on his or her mini-flashcard form. When the sheet is filled with words, the student earns a reward and can take the flashcards home for practice and review. The reward might be a star, sticker or being first in line.

WORD CHARTS
Gorilla Reading Goup

WORD CHARTS
Kangaroo Reading Group

Keep the mini-flashcard worksheets in a file folder so you can locate them quickly. When students keep mini-flashcards in their desk, they get wrinkled and/or lost!

- Before duplicating the mini-flashcard worksheet, write a reading vocabulary word on each card. Students can take the sheet home, cut it apart and use the mini-flashcards for practice.

look	I	see
can	a	am
me	fix	ran
when	man	baby
her	at	home
where	run	there
the	that	mat
fun	top	cat
cup	big	go

Mini-flashcards work well for math facts and spelling words too!

FS-8303 Instant Idea Book

Reading for Meaning

The following pages are chock full of reading comprehension activities
guaranteed to reinforce skills and add excitement to your reading program.
Class discussions and reading aloud give students the opportunity to analyze
what they read in a group setting while worksheet activities encourage
the development of specific comprehension skills. Add a few of your own
creative ideas and you'll always have a variety of stimulating reading activities
to choose from!

Reading reinforcement

READING ALOUD . . .

Give students plenty of opportunity to demonstrate their success in reading.

Reading Partners

- Assign each student to a reading partner. Partners scatter around the classroom and take turns reading a page from the basal reader. The teacher moves from pair to pair. If you have an odd number of students, make a threesome.

Reading to Important People

- If school policy permits, allow students to take basal readers home and reread a story to parents or siblings.

- Arrange with a teacher at a lower grade level to allow one of your students to go into his or her classroom and read to a group or to the class.

- Schedule an appointment for one of your students to read to another teacher, the school librarian, school nurse, school secretary or school administrator.

Reading reinforcement

Everyone Joins In

- When students are reading aloud in a reading circle, tell them that you will snap your fingers from time to time. When you do this, everyone in the group has to read the next word (or sentence) aloud in unison. This keeps everyone involved while one child is reading.

Spell It

- Train your students to spell unfamiliar reading words aloud and continue on with the sentence. Most children will recognize the word before they finish spelling it or as soon as they read the next word or two. By continuing to read, the flow of the sentence is not broken and the word is usually recognized from context.

©Frank Schaffer Publications, Inc. FS-8303 Instant Idea Book

Techniques for meaningful discussions

DISCUSSIONS . . .

Story discussions increase comprehension and oral language skills. Students learn best when they are involved in reading programs that emphasize actual reading and group discussions.

Some techniques for effective group discussions:

Student Questions

● Use student-created comprehension questions for class discussions. (See page 35.)

No Clues

● Break the habit of calling on a student before asking a question. For example, don't say, "Kim, how do you think Mother is feeling in the story?" When you cue the group that Kim is the student you are calling on, the rest of the group can "tune out." Instead, say, "How do you think Mother is feeling in the story?" Then pause for a few seconds before calling on a student. Every child in the group will formulate an answer because no one knows who will be asked to respond.

Pick a Name

● Instead of calling on students who raise their hands, pick names out of an envelope or box. This increases overall class participation.

It's your turn, Kim.

Kim

Names

✓ Techniques for meaningful discussions

Time to Think

● Tell students that you do not want them to raise their hands when you ask a question. Instead, you will ask a question and then say, "Time to think!" Silently count to five. Then call on students to respond. You will find that students who did not participate before will now do so because they had a moment to think before the question was answered by someone else. Student responses will also reflect more thought. An extra plus is that you'll ask better questions because the pace of the discussion will be slower.

Web of Ideas

● Use the chalkboard to cluster ideas about a story. For example, if students read a story about a lost dog who has three adventures before returning home, write on the chalkboard:

Elicit details about the dog's adventures from students and list them under each heading. Students can refer to information on the board for writing sentences or paragraphs, drawing pictures, contrasting and comparing two major events, making a roll movie, etc.

Questions that enhance comprehension

Story Comprehension Questions

There are two types of questions that enhance story comprehension. You should ask both literal and interpretive questions during every story discussion.

LITERAL QUESTIONS: *easy to create and easy for students to answer*

who
what
where
when
how many
how old
what time
definitions for vocabulary words
synonyms for vocabulary words
antonyms for vocabulary words

INTERPRETIVE QUESTIONS: *usually more than one right answer or open-ended*

Main idea: Think of another title for the story.
　　　　　　 What is the story mainly about?
Predicting outcomes: What will happen next?
Drawing conclusions/inferences: How do you think the character feels?
　　　　　　　　　　　　　　　 Why did the character act that way?
　　　　　　　　　　　　　　　 Do you think the character will do that again?
Problem solving: Name two ways the character could solve that problem.
　　　　　　　　 What would you do if you were the character?
　　　　　　　　 How could that situation have been avoided?

Save the questions you use by jotting them down on 5″ x 8″ index cards. Just write the story title and page numbers at the top of each card. When another group is ready to read that story, you have questions ready to go! Saves time and work!

Questions can be used in several ways:

- Write on chalkboard for students to answer on paper.

- Use in oral discussions.

- Use on reading comprehension worksheets.

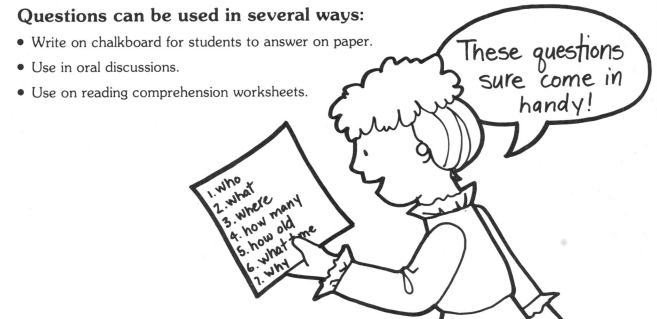

Questions that enhance comprehension

Student-Created Comprehension Questions

Put your students to work! Tell them to write three questions about the story they read in the basal reader. (You might ask older students to write five factual and three interpretive questions.)

How to use student-created questions:

- Each student exchanges papers with a partner. The questions and answers must be written in complete sentences. Student who created the questions checks the answers.

- After students exchange questions and write their answers, have them skim through the story in the basal reader and write the page number where the answer can be found. A great way to develop skimming skills!

- Use the student-created questions in an oral discussion. Students bring their written questions to the discussion group. The same question may not be read aloud twice. This encourages students to think of unusual or unique questions.

- Save the questions to reuse with another reading group. Students can do the activities listed above with questions created by a different group of students.

Students can develop questions to use with science and social studies texts too!

Language Experience Activities

Use language experience activities with basal reader stories.

Instead of having students read a basal reader story, you read it to the group. Then follow up the story with a language experience chart or story.

After your group hears the story, ask each student to dictate a sentence that relates an event from the story. Write the sentences on a large piece of chart paper. Sentences provided by different students result in a group story.

OR

Have individual students dictate their own version of the story you read from the basal reader. Individual stories can be stapled into booklets and placed in the classroom library.

The group language experience chart or individual stories can be used for:
- rereading
- story discussion
- vocabulary
- sentence writing skills
- capitalization/punctuation

Use the workbook pages that accompany the story in the usual manner.

This is also an excellent activity for non-readers. Use picture books from the school library instead of basal readers.

Ungroup for a Day

Break away from your reading groups once in a while and ungroup! Introduce vocabulary words from a story that no one has read yet to the entire class. Allow each student to read the story with a partner. Then have a large-group discussion. Follow-up activities and worksheets can be geared to small-group needs. It is enjoyable to read and discuss a story with the entire class as a pleasant change from the daily routine of the reading program. Try this idea three or four times during the school year to add some variety to your program.

Sequencing Activities

Three terrific activities that require absolutely no preparation time!

- Save newspaper comic strips (such as "Peanuts©") from your Sunday newspaper. Give one cartoon strip to each student. Students cut apart their cartoon strips and exchange scrambled cartoons with a partner. Students must paste the strip in sequence on paper. Students give their pasted comic strips back to the student who cut it apart for checking.

- Have students write three sentences about the story they read. The first sentence tells what happened at the beginning of the story. The second sentence is about the middle of the story. The third sentence tells how the story ended.

- After reading a story in the basal reader, ask students to dictate events that happened in the story. Elicit the events in any order. You might ask for something that happened at the end of the story, then something that happened at the beginning. As students relate events, write each one in sentence form on a strip of paper. Give each strip to a student, who holds it up in front of the entire group. Call on class members to tell students where to move so strips will be arranged in the proper sequence.

Understanding parts of a story

Character Handprints

Give each student a piece of 12" x 18" light-colored construction paper. Students trace their right and left hands, then write the name of an important character from a basal reader story on each handprint. Then they write a detail about that character on each finger.
Another variation is to write an event on each hand and details about the event on each finger.

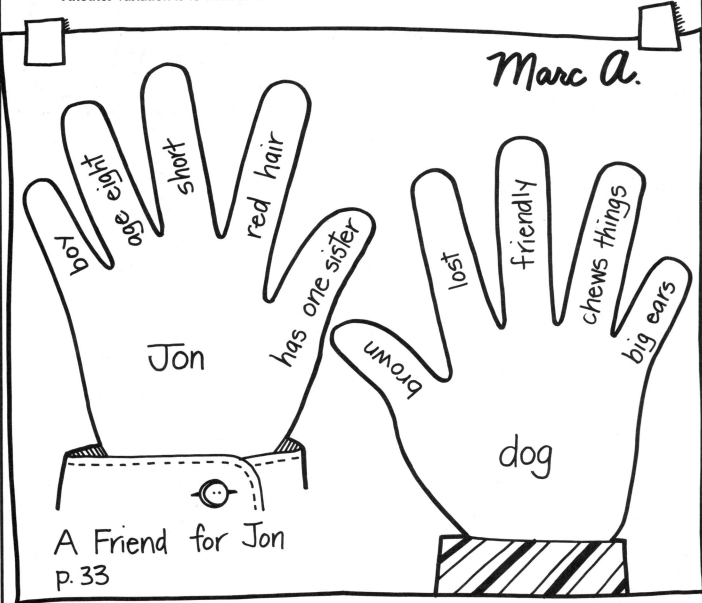

Story Summary & Main Idea

It is easy to summarize a story when you follow a formula. Give each student a copy of the Story Summary worksheet (see page 39). When students make up another title for the story, they are thinking about the main idea.

Name: ______________________________

Story Title: ______________________________

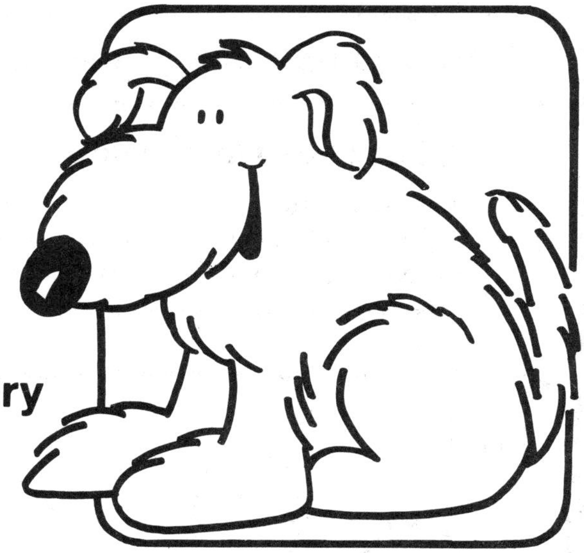

Story Summary

1. Make up a new title for the story.

____

2. Write a sentence about the main character.

____

____

3. What is happening (or what is the problem) in the story?

____

____

4. How is the situation in the story solved?

____

____

5. What happens at the end of the story?

____

____

____

____

Stimulating student involvement

Cut and Paste Sentences

A student-created activity!

Each student selects an interesting sentence from a story in the basal reader. Students copy their sentences on strips of paper and then cut them apart, word by word. The word papers are scrambled and then exchanged with a partner. The partner must paste the sentence in sequence on a piece of 12″ x 18″ paper and draw a picture to illustrate what is happening in the sentence.

Student Response Cards

Children learn more in reading programs that allow for:
• adequate time spent on actual reading.
• time spent discussing what students have read.

One technique for increasing class participation is to give each student a card marked "yes" on one side and "no" on the other (or "true" and "false"). The teacher, or a student, asks a question or makes a statement about the story. All the students respond by holding up the correct side of their cards.

A great way to elicit responses, receive instant feedback and eliminate paperwork!

This works great for syllables: 1 2 3
initital consonants: m P b
ending consonants: P m t
vowel sounds: a e i o u
blends: sh ch
plurals: s es

Stimulating student involvement

Reading Activity Charts

Use with basal reading texts.

The reading activity charts on page 42-45 can be used in a variety of ways:

- Keep the charts as a reference list of ideas.

- Duplicate one or more charts and staple them inside student reading folders. You can assign specific activities to individual students or permit students to choose activities from the charts in their folders.

- My favorite use for reading activity charts not only saves you time and work, but also adds pizzazz to your program. Take a few moments to copy each chart on a large piece of tagboard or butcher paper. Post the charts on a classroom wall or bulletin board and leave them up until you retire. Give assignments to your students by referring to the numbered activities listed on the charts (see illustration). The charts are especially handy when you have a substitute. Just indicate the appropriate activity numbers on your lesson plans.

bulletin board ↗

Add your favorite activities to each chart.

Reading Aloud

R1   Take turns reading the story aloud with your partner.

R2   Read the part of the story you like best to your partner.

R3   Read the most exciting part of the story to your partner.

R4   Read the funniest part of the story to your partner.

R5   Read sentences from the story that tell what happened at the beginning, middle and end. Read to your partner.

R6   Read a part of the story that describes an important character. Read to your partner.

R7   Read what an important character from the story said. Read to your partner.

R8   Read a part of the story that describes the setting. Read to your partner.

R9   Practice reading a page from the story. Read it to the group.

R10   Take turns reading flashcards with your partner.

FS-8303 Instant Idea Book

Ralph
1. happy 2. curious 3. small
Tabby
1. yellow 2. agile 3. friendly
Pete
1. bashful 2. blond 3. short
Jim C.

RALPH

Word Skills

W1 Write the names of all the important characters in the story. Write 3 words to describe each character.

W2 List 10 two-syllable and 5 three-syllable words from the story.

W3 Write 10 words from the story in ABC order.

W4 List 10 words from the story. Write a synonym for each word.

W5 List 10 words from the story. Write an antonym for each word.

W6 Make flashcards for important words in the story.

W7 List 10 words from the story that have prefixes or suffixes. Underline the root words.

W8 List 10 words from the story. Rewrite them as plurals.

W9 Skim the story. Make a list of compound words.

W10 Skim the story. List words that tell **who**, **when**, and **where**.

FS-8303 Instant Idea Book

Understanding What You Read

U1 Write 8 statements about the story. Make some true and some false. Give your statements to a partner who has read the story. Check the worksheet after it has been completed.

U2 Write 5 questions about the story. You will ask your questions during our class dicussion.

U3 Write a paragraph that summarizes the story.

U4 Write 5 sentences that describe where the story takes place.

U5 Write 5 multiple-choice questions about the story. Make sure that only one answer choice is correct for each question.

U6 Draw a picture that shows the main idea of the story. Write a new title for the story above the picture.

U7 Write 6 events that happened in the story. Write them out of order. Have a partner number the events in order. Check the answers.

U8 Retell the story in your own words.

U9 Write about an experience you have had that is similar to an experience in the story.

U10 List all the characters from the story. Write a sentence to describe each character.

Last night the first snow fell.

Sue made three large balls of snow.

A jolly snowman soon stood outside.

Enrichment Activities

E1 Draw 3 pictures that show events from the beginning, middle and end of the story. Write a sentence that describes each picture.

E2 Write a different ending for the story.

E3 Write a note to your teacher. Describe what you liked best or least about the story.

E4 Make puppets of two characters from the story.

E5 Make a roll movie about the story.

E6 Make 2 bookmarks about the story.

E7 Make a poster about the story.

E8 Make a mural about the story with a partner.

E9 Make a word hunt using words from the story. Use graph paper.

E10 Make a crossword puzzle using words from the story. Use graph paper.

FS-8303 Instant Idea Book

How to use reading worksheets

Reading Report Worksheets

How to use the reproducible worksheets on pages 47-49:

One page at a time . . .

Give each student a copy of the Reading Time Schedule to keep track of progress in silent reading.

Use one or both of these worksheets as a follow-up activity for a basal reader story.

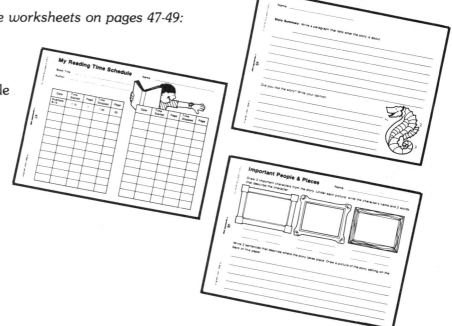

Make an activity packet . . .

Staple all three pages together for each student.* Add a construction paper cover. Students can draw a new cover for the book or story. This packet can be used in your book report program, for required or extra-credit reading.

*Duplicate worksheets and let students collate and staple their own packets.

My Reading Time Schedule

Name: _____

Book Title: _____

Author: _____

Date	Time Started	Page	Time Stopped	Page

Date	Time Started	Page	Time Stopped	Page
Example: 9/15	1:15	1	1:40	20

a reproducible page

FS-8303 Instant Idea Book

Name: _____

Important People & Places

Draw 3 important characters from the story. Under each picture, write the character's name and 2 words that describe the character.

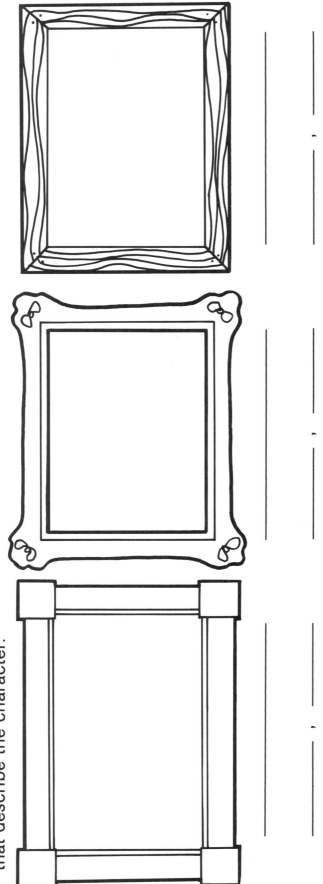

_____ , _____

_____ , _____

_____ , _____

Write 2 sentences that describe where the story takes place. Draw a picture of the story setting on the back of this paper.

_____
_____
_____
_____
_____

48
a reproducible page

FS-8303 Instant Idea Book

Name ______________________

Story Summary: Write a paragraph that tells what the story is about.

Did you like the story? Write your opinion.

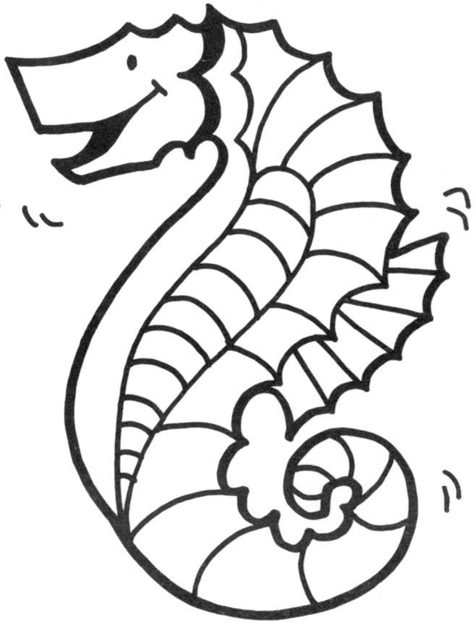

My ideas for reading comprehension . . .

50

Reading Activities

Use your imagination and the creative ideas on the following pages to add variety and fun to reading time in your classroom. Spice up book reports, learn how to use grids for visual skills and play story-related games. Students will develop a positive attitude about reading while acquiring valuable skills.

Developing visual skills

Visual Skills Grids

for grades K-6

This activity is excellent for visual skills development as well as practice and review of word skills. Plus, it takes care of one of your bulletin boards all year long!

Use a felt tip pen to draw a grid on a large piece of butcher paper (approximately 36″ x 40″). The difficulty level of your grid should be appropriate for your students.

Some sample grids . . .

K-1

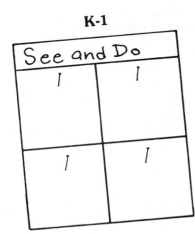

K-2

1-3

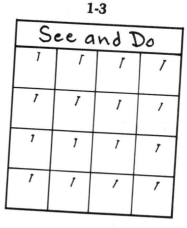

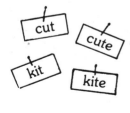

Post the grid on a bulletin board and poke a pin in each square. When you want to post a word on the grid, write the word on a card and hang it on the pin. Your grid can be changed quickly and easily by simply hanging up new word cards.

2-6

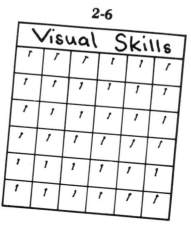

Make reproducible answer sheets for students to use. To save paper, make answer sheets on tagboard and laminate. Students can wipe off and reuse the laminated answer cards.

Answer sheets . . .

More ideas on next page. →

FS-8303 Instant Idea Book

Developing visual skills

How to use the visual skills grid . . .

Leave the grid on the bulletin board all year. Change the word cards weekly or daily. Cards are easy to put up and take down if you punch a hole in them and hang the cards on the pin. When you remove the cards, store them in an envelope or put a rubber band around them and store them in a shoe box. They can be reused next year.

Students must make their answer sheets look like your grid or they must write their answers in the appropriate squares on their answer sheets. Make sure you explain the directions for each activity so students can concentrate on the task at hand instead of wasting time wondering what they are supposed to do.

For example: If you post contraction word cards on the grid, students must write the two words for each contraction in the appropriate square on their answer sheets.

Idea! Leave a few squares blank. This makes the task more difficult visually.

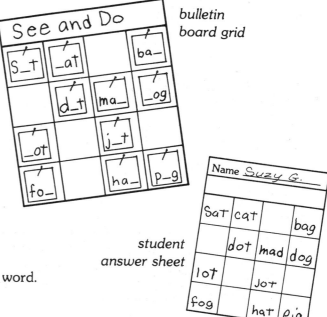

bulletin board grid

student answer sheet

Ideas for skill cards:

Use words from reading or spelling vocabulary.

Students copy words and do activity or write answer in the appropriate squares on the answer sheets.

Ideas:

- mark short or long vowels.
- mark vowels and cross out silent letter.
- write the dictionary pronunciation for each word.
- divide the words into syllables.
- make each word plural.
- add suffixes.
- add prefixes.
- change words to past tense.
- read color words on the grid and color the appropriate squares on their answer sheets.
- read number words on the grid and write numerals in the appropriate squares on their answer sheets.
- write synonyms for words on the grid.
- write antonyms for words on the grid.
- write rhyming words for words on the grid.
- write the alphabet letter that comes between letters on the grid. (For example: If you write "m __ o" on the grid, students write "n" in the matching square on their answer sheets.)
- write the number that comes between numbers on the grid.
- write the answer to math problems on the grid (addition, subtraction, multiplication, division, reduce fractions, rewrite improper fractions).
- copy shapes from the grid using the same color.

Tools of the trade

Factual Bookmarks

Cut enough strips of 3″ x 12″ light-colored construction paper for everyone in your class. Write the name of a different state on each strip, then give one strip to each student.

> **CARSON, Rachel** 1907-1964
> She was a marine biologist and science writer.

> **CARTER, Jimmy** 1924-
> He was the 39th president of the United States.

Students look up the state that is written on their bookmarks and write information about the state. For example, students can write the name of the state's capital city, draw and color the state bird, flower and flag, etc.

Collect the student-made bookmarks and donate them to the school library, another class or keep them in your own classroom library for students to use. Your class can make additional sets of factual bookmarks using:

PLACES: a sentence telling the location and why the place is famous or important.
PEOPLE: dates of birth/death and a sentence telling why the person is famous or important.
INVENTIONS: inventor's name and a sentence telling how the invention is used or why it is important.
WORDS: dictionary pronunciation and definition of an unusual word.

Finding the Facts

If you have a set of encyclopedias in your classroom, write several questions on a card and paste a different card inside the front cover of each volume. Write questions that can be answered by looking up information in that volume. For young students, you might want to indicate the page number where the answer will be found or underline key word to be looked up. The answer to each question should appear in the first few sentences under that heading in in the encyclopedia. Students may write answers to the encyclopedia questions during free time or for extra-credit points.

Underline the word the student must look up to make the task simpler.

From time to time, read one of the questions aloud. Call on a child who knows the answer to share it with the class. If no one knows the answer, tell the class where to find the answer in the encyclopedia.

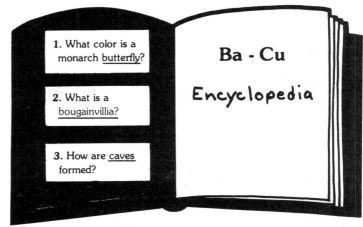

1. What color is a monarch <u>butterfly</u>?

2. What is a <u>bougainvillia</u>?

3. How are <u>caves</u> formed?

Ba - Cu

Encyclopedia

Successful book reports

Book Report Activities

Use the book report activities on the following pages to create a high-interest program for your students. Write each activity on a 5" x 8" card. Punch a hole in each card and slip on binder rings. Make three sets of cards:

- Write About Your Book
- Talk About Your Book
- Make Something About Your Book

You can assign specific activities or permit individual students to select an activity. You may want to require each student to complete at least one activity from each set of cards during the school year.

When you read about or think of another book report activity, simply write it on a card and add it to the appropriate set of activity cards.

Communicate with Parents

Inform parents of due dates for book reports. Send a sign-and-return note home with students or give parents your book report schedule during the first parent conference of the school year. Parents want to be informed and will be pleased that you shared this information with them.

Dear Parents,

Six book reports are required in fourth grade. Students must read one fairy tale, one biography, one animal book, two fiction books and one book of their choice.

Due dates for the book reports are:

October 14
December 15
January 30
March 5
April 15
June 1

Books may be read in any order. Please make a note of this information. Kindly sign this note and have your child bring it to school tomorrow.

Mrs. Gruber

Parent _____

Successful book reports

Write About Your Book

- Pretend that you are an important character in the story. Write a diary for one week.

- Write a letter to the author of the book. Tell him or her your opinion of the story, characters, etc.

- Write a letter about the book to your school librarian. Summarize the story and include your opinion of the book.

- Write a letter about the book to your school principal.

- Write a different ending for the story.

- Write a paragraph to describe an important character in the story. Draw a portrait of the character you wrote about.

- Pretend that you are a newspaper reporter. Write a news article about the book you read. Your article should include the basic facts: who, what, where, when, why and how.

- Write about an important event in the story. Tell what happened, where, when, to whom and why.

- Write a description of the story setting. Draw a picture of the setting to accompany your written description.

- Make a list of the main characters in the story. Write two sentences to describe each character.

- If your book is about a famous person, write about that person. Tell why he or she is famous, three or more things you learned about the person and which part of his or her life was most interesting to you.

- Write a letter to a classmate telling why he/she should or should not read the book.

- Write a list of reasons why you liked or disliked the book.

- Write a poem about the book.

- Make a crossword puzzle or word hunt using the words from the story.

- Write a script for an exciting part of the story. Act out the script with your classmates.

Successful book reports

Talk About Your Book

- Have a private talk with your teacher about the book.

- Act out an exciting scene from the book.

- Present a radio announcement to advertise the book.
  Tell listeners why they will or will not enjoy reading the book.

- Read an exciting part of the book to your class or to a group of students.

- Pretend that you are a character in the book. Tell the story in your own words. Dress up like that character.

- Give an oral report. Read the title of another book by the same author. If possible, show copies of both books.

- Describe two events from the book that are funny, sad, exciting, scary, happy or interesting.

- If your book tells how to do or make something, give a demonstration to show what you have learned.

- Pretend that you are a news reporter filing a report during an exciting part of the story.

- Tell the class about an event that happened at the beginning, middle and end of the story.

- Tell the class how the book ended. Describe how you would have ended the story if you had been the author.

My book report is about <u>The Pilgrims</u>.

THE PILGRIMS

FS-8303 Instant Idea Book

Successful book reports

Make Something About Your Book

- Make a new book jacket. Write a summary of the story for inside flap of your book jacket.

- Draw a scene that illustrates the main idea of the book. Write two sentences to describe the main idea.

- Make two or more puppets (stick puppets, finger puppets or paper bag puppets) to represent characters from the book. Put on a puppet show of an exciting part of the story.

- Make a roll movie of the events in the book.

- Make a shoe box diorama to show an interesting or exciting scene from the book.

- Fold a piece of 12″ x 18″ white drawing paper in half three times to make eight sections. Use a ruler to draw lines that divide the sections. Draw handwriting lines in the first section and write the book title and author. Draw colorful pictures about the story in the remaining seven sections.

- Make a series of three pictures to show an event that happened at the beginning, middle and end of the book.

- Make three bookmarks about the book. Show a main character, an important scene and the main idea of the book.

- Make a poster to advertise the book.

- Make a map to show the setting of the story. Label your map to indicate where important events happened.

- Make a time line to show important events from the story.

- Make a pocket-sized book about the story for a friend. Your book should include the main characters, the setting and a story summary.

- Draw a mural to illustrate the book.

- Make a cartoon strip about the book.

Finger
Puppet

FS-8303 Instant Idea Book

Successful book reports

Book Report Center

Set it up to use throughout the year!

Have book report forms available (see pages 60 and 61) for students. Students select a book to read for an extra-credit book report. After reading the book, the student fills out a book report form. Upon completion of each book report, the student's name is written on a railroad car and added to the book report train.

Use the patterns below to make a locomotive from black construction paper. Duplicate railroad cars on bright-colored construction paper. The book report train can chug along a bulletin board or classroom wall. Students enjoy watching the train grow!

BOOK REPORTS
1. Choose a book to read
2. Do a book report
3. Your name will be added to our train!

BOOK REPORT FORMS

FINISHED REPORTS

Ask students to let you know when book report forms are running low.

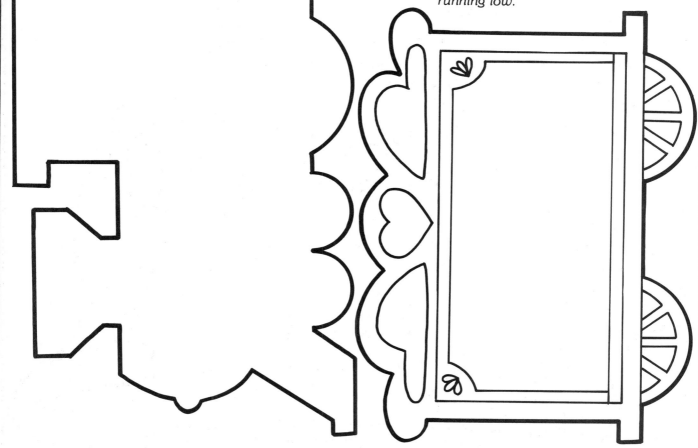

FS-8303 Instant Idea Book

My Book Report

Title: _____

Author: _____

Draw a picture about the story.

Write a sentence about the story.

_____
_____
_____

Book Report Form - Primary

FS-8303 Instant Idea Book

My Book Report

Name ______________________

Title: ______________________

Author: ______________________ Type: ☐ fiction ☐ nonfiction

Important Characters:

____

Setting: Write a sentence telling where the story takes place.

____

____

Plot: Write a summary of the story.

____

____

____

____

____

____

____

____

Evaluation: Did you like the book? Describe why or why not.

____

____

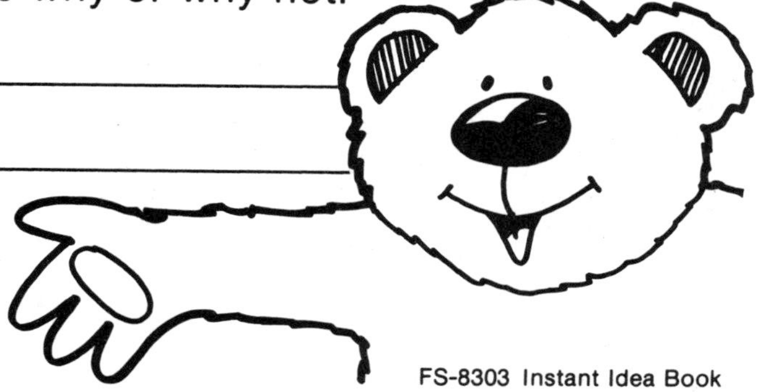

Book Report Form - Intermediate

First Weeks of School

1. Label objects — Write messages. P.6
2. Silent rdg. — Use picture books.
3. Book Talks — P.10 Use with picture books.
4. Do Finger Plays + Poetry
5. Student Created books — P.12
6. P.13 — Color + Alphabet books, also numbers
7. Class book — Show film on a subject — Draw picture + then take child's dictation. P.15
8. Illustrate vocabulary words — P.21
9. Print vocab. words on paper. — P.27
10. P.31 — Reading reinforcement
11. P.36 — Lang. Ex. — Rd. story — Each person tells you a sentence about the story. Do on chart rack.

 **My ideas for vocabulary building . . .**

28

FS-8303 Instant Idea Book

Mini-Flashcard Format